Facts About

Families

DONNA BAILEY

STECK-VAUGHN LIBRARY
Austin, Texas

How to Use This Book

This book tells you many things about families all around the world. There is a Table of Contents on the next page. It shows you what each double page of the book is about. For example, pages 10 and 11 tell you about "Large Families."

On many of these pages you will find some words that are printed in **bold** type. The bold type shows you that these words are in the Glossary on pages 46 and 47. The Glossary explains the meaning of some words that may be new to you.

At the very end of the book there is an Index. The Index tells you where to find certain words in the book. For example, you can use it to look up words like foster parents, households, relatives, and many other words to do with families.

Published in the United States in 1990 by Steck-Vaughn Co., Austin, Texas, a subsidiary of National Education Corporation.

Material used in this book first appeared in Macmillan World Library: *Families Around the World*. Published by Macmillan Children's Books

Printed and bound in the United States
1 2 3 4 5 6 7 8 9 0 LB 94 93 92 91 90

Library of Congress Cataloging-in-Publication Data

Bailey, Donna.
Families / Donna Bailey.
p. cm. — (Facts about)
Summary: Describes different types of families around the world, discusses how families work and play together, and defines such terms as foster parent, household, and relative.
ISBN 0-8114-2514-2
1. Family — Juvenile literature. [1. Family. 2. Family life.]
I. Title. II. Series: Facts about (Austin, Tex.) 89-29332
HQ516.B26 1990 CIP
306.85—dc20 AC

Contents

Introduction

this Indian girl helps her father sell oranges in the market

A family is a group of people who are **related** to each other. Children in a family are taken care of until they can take care of themselves.

Some families are small. Others can be very large.

In some countries, all the related people in a big family live together. They help each other and work together in the home.

In other countries, only the parents and children live together, until the children leave to find work or get married.

Many people choose not to marry, but to live alone or with friends.

a family in their home
in West Africa

a family at the beach

Animal Families

Animals act by **instinct** when they produce their young, or when they learn how to escape from danger.

Insects lay hundreds of eggs, but they do not care for them at all. When this African moth has finished laying her eggs, she will fly away and leave the eggs to hatch by themselves.

Birds lay eggs too, but they look after the eggs and keep them warm. When the eggs **hatch**, birds care for their young and teach them to find food. After five months these young **cygnets** will leave the parent swans to go and take care of themselves.

laying eggs on a twig

adult swans care for the cygnets

Mammals are animals that do not lay eggs, but which give birth to their young.

Chimpanzees and human beings are both mammals. Chimps live in friendly groups, and a baby chimp learns from its mother and the members of the group.

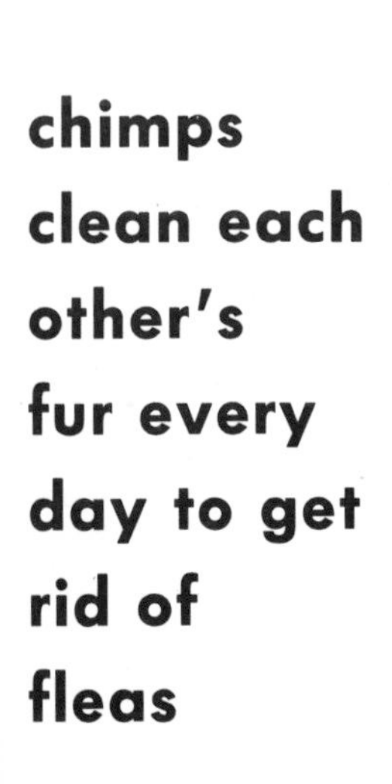

chimps clean each other's fur every day to get rid of fleas

Human Families

The smallest family group is one parent or grown-up and a child.

Many children grow up in this kind of family if one of the parents has died or if the parents are **divorced**.

Some people **adopt** children whose parents cannot care for them. Other children sometimes live with **foster parents**.

the whole family goes shopping together

Every small family is part of a larger one, which includes cousins, grandparents, aunts, and uncles, who are the closest relatives.

Some people live and grow up with many of their relatives and the family does many things together.

these English children live in different kinds of families

Large Families

Some large family groups or **households** live and work together.

This family in south India lives in a group of houses called a **compound**. When the children grow up and marry, they will still live in the compound. The household can become very large. The grandfather is the head of the family.

The Muslim **religion** allows men to have more than one wife.

The picture shows a man in northern Nigeria with five wives and their children. All his wives are treated the same.

Having more than one wife at the same time is called **polygamy**. Most Muslims now choose to have only one wife.

Feeding the Family

All families need food and clothes. People in different parts of the world work in different ways to get the food they need.

The picture shows a family in Greece helping to mend fishing nets. Greece has many islands, so a lot of Greek people own fishing boats and go out to catch fish to eat.

caring for the goats and sheep

This little boy helps care for the goats that give his family meat to eat and milk to drink. It is very dry where he lives in northern Pakistan. There are few plants for the animals to eat so his family moves around from place to place to find food for their goats.

In China, parents who work in factories can leave their young children in **nurseries** during the day while they are at work. Then the parents can earn money to buy food and clothes for their families.

caring for the children

Working Away from Home

In many families the parents leave home to work and earn money. Sometimes if their jobs are not too far away, they can cycle to work.

These women in Botswana build houses while the men tend cattle.

cycling to work in Beijing, China

women in Botswana

The men in Botswana leave their homes for part of the year to find land with good **grazing** for their cattle.

In other countries men leave their families to find jobs in the cities.

The picture shows workers on an oil rig off the coast of Scotland. The men work hard and earn a lot of money to send home to their families. They don't go home often.

Working at Home

This woman lives in the Sudan. She is grinding grain with a stone to make flour. She wets the grain as she grinds it. This makes dough that she bakes to make bread for her family to eat. Other jobs are done at home as well as cooking and cleaning.

weaving in the Andes

In the Andes the women dye the wool from animals and weave rugs and blankets.

People in other places make pottery, lace, and baskets that they sell.

Many people do not have to travel to work.
They work from home and use computers, telephones, and **facsimile** machines to keep in touch with others.

working at home

Houses and Apartments

People build their homes out of all sorts of **materials**, like mud or clay. They often use what materials they can find near the village.

These people live on an island in Lake Titicaca in South America. They make the walls of their homes from the reeds that grow nearby.

houses in Australia

Many houses in Australia are **single-story** houses, each with its own garden. They are built of brick, with tiled roofs.

Lots of people in cities live in **multistory** apartments because there is no space to build separate houses. They do not have gardens, and often apartments are crowded with many relatives living together.

Some apartments have thick walls and shutters on the windows to keep them cool. Inside there are stairs up to each apartment.

Other apartments have elevators and **air-conditioning**.

multistory apartments

Different Homes

The size and shape of different homes depends on where people live.

These houses in the fishing village of Rio Hondo in the Philippines are built above the ground on **stilts** to protect them from floods.
The people travel around in their boats to visit their neighbors.

These homes in Tanzania have thick mud walls and thatched roofs to keep the houses cool.
The woman is drying corn cobs for the winter on a platform beside the house.

Some houses have many appliances to help with the work in the home.
How many appliances can you see in the picture?

making pancakes

Different Religions

Some religions make rules about how people should live, what they should wear, and what they should eat. When people follow a particular religion, it is often part of their everyday life.

Muslims must pray fives times a day. When they say their prayers, they stop what they are doing and kneel to face their holy city of Mecca.

a Muslim saying prayers in the desert

a Jewish family

Many religions have a sacred day in the week.

For Jews it is Saturday, the Sabbath. Families come together on Friday evening for a meal on the eve of the Sabbath.

Hindus believe that the cow is a sacred animal, so nobody is allowed to stop cows walking in the street.

a cow in an Indian street

Weddings

When people get married
a wedding ceremony
takes place.

In the Soviet Union, many
people do not practice a
religion, so they don't
have a service before
a priest in a church.
But the bride may still wear
a traditional white dress.

a Soviet wedding

The bride and groom at a
Japanese wedding both wear
traditional clothes.
The bride wears a
colorful **kimono**.
The wedding guests wear
their dress suits and
nicest clothes.

a wedding in Japan

a Hindu wedding

At this Hindu wedding, the bride wears a **sari** and a lot of jewelry and her husband is dressed in white. There are flowers everywhere and they both have garlands of flowers around their necks.

They eat a special wedding meal.

Special Days

Most families think birthdays are special days. This family is **celebrating** their son's first birthday. He has a special birthday cake with one candle on it.

Christian families celebrate Christmas. This family is opening their presents under the decorated Christmas tree.

This Jewish boy is reading to his family and friends from the Torah, the holy writings of Judaism, during his *Bar Mitzvah*.
He will then be blessed by the **rabbi**.
It is the first Sabbath after his thirteenth birthday.

After his Bar Mitzvah he is thought of as a grown-up and can take part in the religious life of the community.

Jewish girls have a similar ceremony called a *Bat Mitzvah*.

The Wider Family

Most families live near other people in a **community** where they speak the same language, and share the same customs and ideas.

The families in this Indonesian fishing community share in the life and work of the community and help each other during times of trouble.

a market in France

Even in towns, people living in the same **neighborhood** can form a community.

Markets help to keep the community together. People meet there to shop and to chat.

In other large cities, people with the same background live together in a community, as in San Francisco's Chinatown.

a Chinese community

Living in Groups

When people live in groups together they make rules about what to do and what not to do.

At this village meeting in West Pakistan, the people have come to talk about how to run the village.

Sometimes the people hold an **election** to choose some leaders who will run their community for them.

These women in Algeria are voting in a local election. They put a cross on a piece of paper beside the names they choose and put their paper into a locked box. When everybody has voted, the papers are sorted and counted to see who has won the most votes and been elected.

Working Together

A commune is a special kind of community, where all the people share the land and the work together. The commune is run by a group of people who plan which crops to grow. They sell the goods to the government.

On this commune in China, one child takes care of two others while the parents work in the fields.

In Israel, a large farm that works like a commune is called a **kibbutz**. The children on a kibbutz spend their day together. They are looked after by "house-mothers" while their parents are at work. At the end of each day, the parents and children spend some time together.

Most of Israel's fruit and vegetables are grown on the many kibbutzim.

children on a kibbutz

a field of tomatoes

Caring for Others

Most people in a family try to take care of each other.
But sometimes the house or apartment may be too small for the grandparents to live with their children.
The grandparents may live in a community with the other older people, like this Japanese grandfather.
His family visits him every week.

fun in the pool

Some elderly people like to live in places where it is warm and sunny. These people live in a home for the elderly and keep fit by swimming.

Most communities take special care of sick and handicapped people.

enjoying a ball game

People Who Help Us

People living in cities and towns can visit the doctor when they are sick. If they are very ill, they go to a hospital where doctors and nurses look after them.

People living in the desert may only see a doctor once a year. Health workers visit them and teach them how to care for themselves.

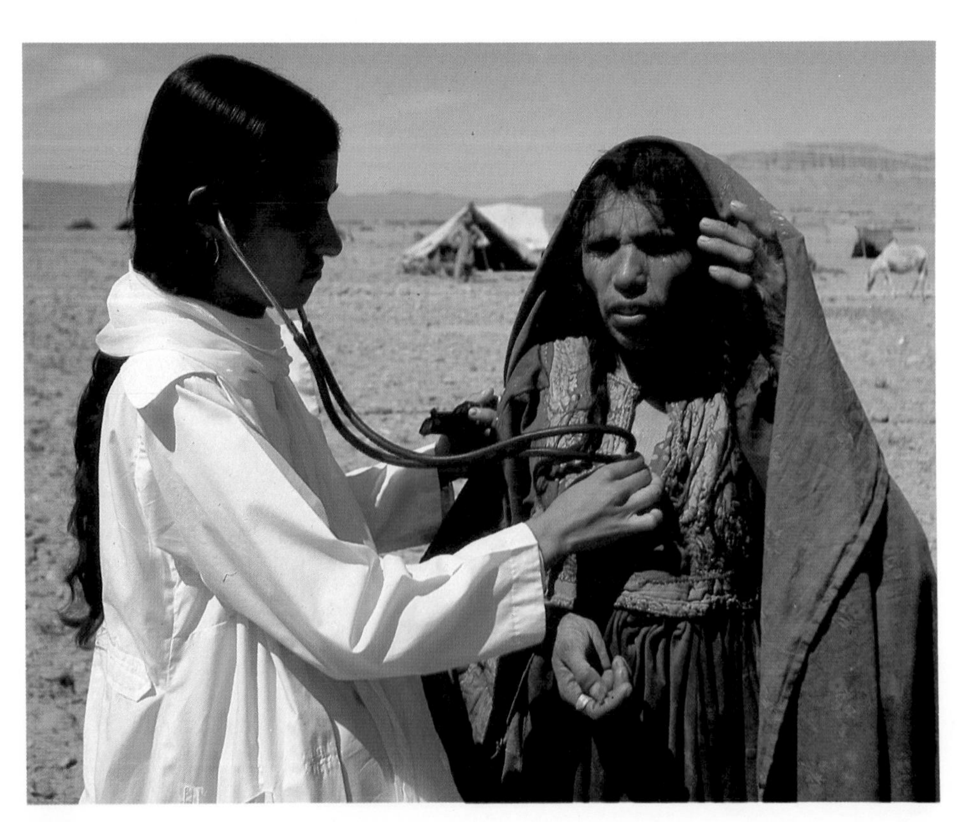

a local library

In many towns and cities, there are libraries for everyone to use. People can borrow books and learn more about the things that interest them.

In some countries teachers train people to use a tractor or to improve their land so they can grow more crops.

Sports and Games

Playing sports and games helps keep you fit.
Families enjoy many different kinds of sports.

The picture shows how families in Prague, Czechoslovakia, enjoy doing exercises together.

a ''fun run'' in Hyde Park, London

Some sports are useful for **self-defense**.
These children are learning karate.
They learn to fight using their legs, heads, hands, and elbows.

a karate class in Korea

Festivals

Most communities have a special day
to celebrate an important event.
Then everybody has a day off, and
there may be a parade.

This picture shows carnival time in
New Orleans, in Louisiana.
Crowds of people watch the carnival
parade and the decorated floats.
The people in the procession dress up
in bright costumes.

carnival in Trinidad

Every year in Trinidad
there is a big carnival.
People dress up in
colorful costumes.
The singing and dancing
goes on all day and night.

A royal wedding is
also a time to celebrate,
like the wedding of Prince
Charles and Lady Diana
Spencer in England.

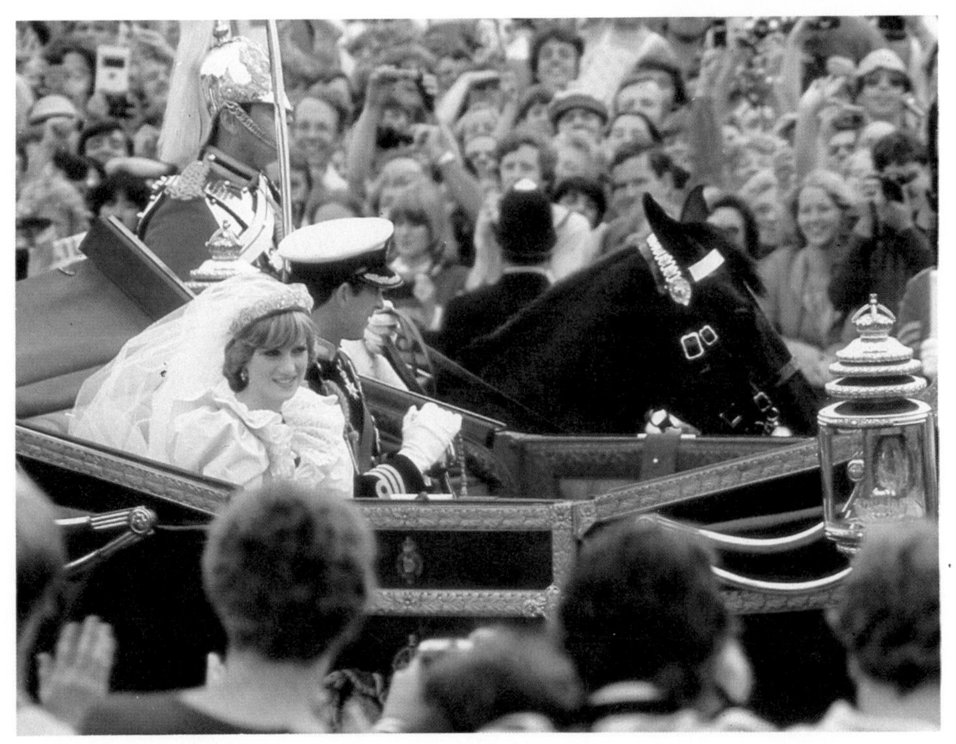

Sharing with Others

In some parts of the world people do not have enough food to eat. If there is a bad drought, the crops cannot grow, and the people starve. The picture shows some people in Ethiopia who have walked for many days to find water to fill their pots.

trucks deliver food to Chad

Sometimes there is too much rain, and then the crops are washed away and the animals are drowned in the floods.

These trucks are taking food to the starving people of Chad.
The roads are bad, and the heavy trucks must be careful when crossing the wooden bridges.
People from all over the world gave money to buy food for Chad.

All One Family

Although we live in very different communities, we all live in the same world and share the same feelings and needs. We are like one big family.

Television helps us understand the problems of people in other lands. We see the effects of droughts, floods, and hurricanes.

We need to help each other
and share the world's food
so that everyone has
enough to eat.

We must also take care
not to destroy the world
we live in by polluting
the air, rivers, and oceans, or
by cutting down the forests.

If we destroy our world,
there will be nothing left
for our children to enjoy,
and the human family will
be much poorer.

Glossary

adopt when people take a child into their family and look after him or her as their own child.
air-conditioning air that is cooled by a machine and is then blown throughout a building to keep it cool.
celebrating having a party to mark a special event such as a wedding.
community a group of people who live and work in the same place.
compound a group of houses surrounded by its own fence or wall.
cygnets young swans.
divorced when a marriage between a man and a woman is legally ended.
election an event when people choose somebody by voting for them.
facsimile a machine that can make exact copies of printed messages or photographs sent by phone.
foster parents people who look after a child while the child's own parents are unable to do so.
grazing fresh grass and food for cattle.
hatch when young birds break out of eggs.
households homes and all the people who live in them.
instinct a way of doing things without having to learn how.
kibbutz a farming community in Israel.
kimono traditional Japanese dress.
mammals animals with warm bodies that are usually covered with fur. Young mammals feed on their mother's milk.
materials different kinds of things used in buildings.
multistory a building with more than one floor.
neighborhood a group of streets that form part of a city or town.
nurseries places where young children are taken care of.
polygamy having more than one wife at the same time.
rabbi a leader in the Jewish religion.
related being a member of a family.
religion a system of beliefs in a god or gods.
sari the traditional dress worn by Indian women.

self-defense defending yourself when under attack.
single-story a building with only one floor.
stilts poles that raise something off the ground to a higher level.

Index

Acknowledgments
The Publishers wish to thank the following organizations for their invaluable assistance in the preparation of this book.
Kuwait Embassy
NASA
Oxfam
Shell

Photographic credits
(t=top b=bottom l=left r=right)
Cover photograph: Colorific!; title page Robert Harding Associates
4 ZEFA; 5*t* The Hutchison Library; 5*b* ZEFA; 6 Anthony Bannister NHPA; 6 7 Brian Hawkes NHPA; 7 Patrick Fagot NHPA; 8 ZEFA; 9*t* Chris Fairclough; 9*b*, 10, 11 The Hutchison Library; 12 ZEFA; 13*t*, 13*b*, 14*t*, 14*b* The Hutchison Library; 15 Shell; 16 The Hutchison Library; 17*t* South American Pictures; 17*b* ZEFA; 18 South American Pictures; 19*l* ZEFA; 19*r* The Hutchison Library; 20 ZEFA; 21*t* The Hutchison Library; 21*b* Macmillan Education; 22, 23*t* 23*b*, 24*t*, 24*b*, 25 ZEFA; 26*t* 26b, 27 The Hutchison Library; 28 Chris Fairclough; 29*t* Douglas Dickens; 29*b* ZEFA; 30 Douglas Dickens; 31, 32, 33*t*, 33*b*, 34 The Hutchison Library; 35*t*, 36*b* ZEFA; 36 The Hutchison Library; 37*t* Kuwait Embassy; 37*b*, 38, 39*t*, 39*b* The Hutchison Library; 40, 41*t* ZEFA; 41*b*, 42, 43 The Hutchison Library; 43 Oxfam; 44 45 NASA